The King Of Egypt - Tutankhamun

Life, Death & Afterlife of The Boy King

Amelie O'Connor

Contents

Introduction

Tutankhamun- the living image of the god Amun) originally known as Tutankhaten- the living image of the god Aten (c. 1341 – c. 1323 BC), commonly referred to as King Tut, was an Egyptian pharaoh who was the last of his royal family to rule during the end of the 18th Dynasty (ruled c. 1332 – 1323 BC in the conventional chronology) during the New Kingdom of Egyptian history.

King Tutankhamun was completely lost from history until his tomb was found in the 1900s. His tomb and mummy are still being examined using high-tech instruments. His brief reign as pharaoh was not very notable, but the 1922 discovery of the Boy King's undamaged tomb (now known as

KV62) by an archaeological expedition headed by British Egyptologist Howard Carter confirmed his position in the history books. But although Tutankhamun's tomb was opulent, historical and archaeological evidence shows that the young king was unwell and spent his brief time attempting to overturn a religious revolution that his father had launched.

King Tutankhamun's spirit is remembered today via his well preserved tomb and the extraordinary objects discovered inside it. The 4th November 2022 celebrates 100 years since British archaeologist Howard Carter unearthed his grave.

Map of Ancient Egypt

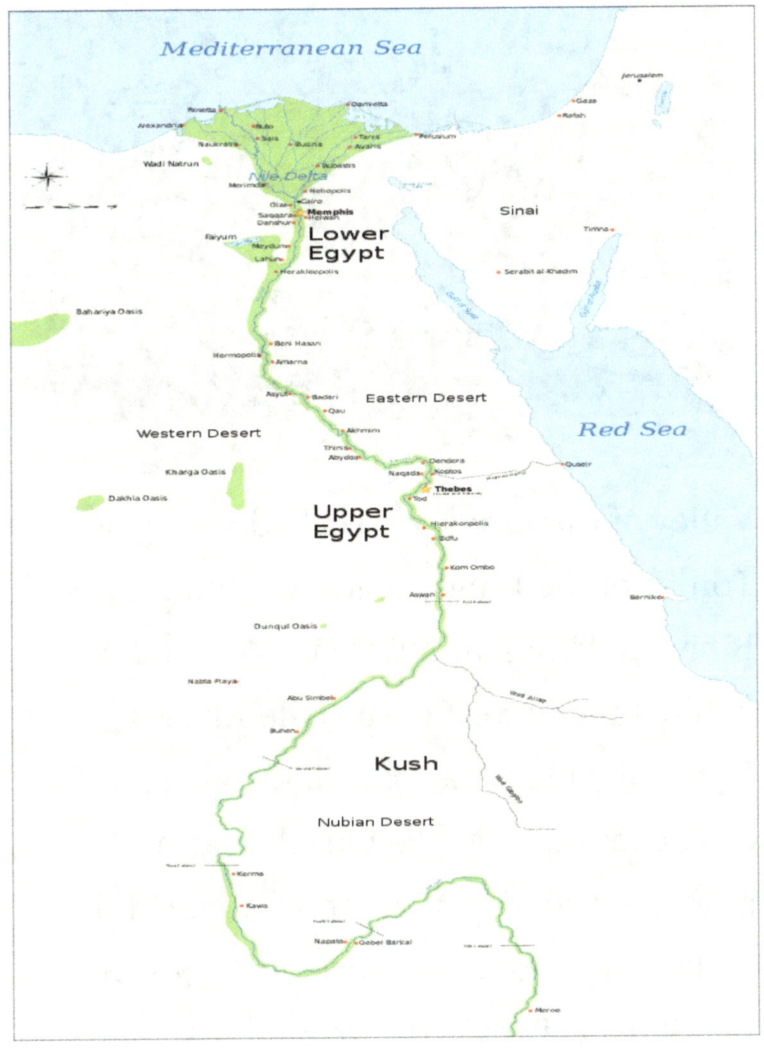

Valley of the kings

Valley of the Kings, also called Valley of the Tombs of the Kings. Wādī Al-Mulūk or Wādī Bībān al-Mulūk in Arabic is a long narrow defile directly west of the Nile River in Upper Egypt. It was part of the ancient city of Thebes and was the burial location of practically all the rulers (pharaohs) of the 18th, 19th, and 20th dynasties (1539–1075 BCE), from Thutmose I to Ramses X.

Located in the hills below Dayr al-Baḥrī, the 62 known tombs demonstrate variation both in layout and in ornamentation.

In 1979 UNESCO recognized the valley as part of the World Heritage site of ancient Thebes.These also includes Luxor, the Valley of the Queens, and Karnak.
The rulers of the New Kingdom (c. 1539–1075 BCE), afraid for the protection of their wealthy graves, established a new method of hiding their tombs in a lonely valley in the western highlands beyond Dayr al-Baḥrī. There, in graves buried deep into the heart of the mountain, pharaohs are laid to rest, as were many queens, a few officials of high rank, and the countless offspring of Ramses II.

The design of the tombs varies widely but consists primarily of a descending hallway broken by deep shafts to confound thieves and by pillared rooms or vestibules. At the end of the passageway is a burial room with a stone sarcophagus in which the royal mummy was preserved and storage chambers around which furnishings and equipment were piled high for the king's use in the next world.

The walls were in many cases covered with sculpted and painted scenes depicting the dead king in the presence of deities, especially the gods of the underworld, and with illustrated magical texts similar to those found in funerary papyri, designed to help him on his journey through the nether regions. There were several books which depict various but not necessarily competing conceptions of the afterlife, in which the monarch had to face trials and conquer hazards. Astronomical motifs cover the ceilings of most burial rooms.

Virtually all of the graves in the valley were wiped away in antiquity. Some had been partly looted during the New Kingdom, but all were methodically denuded of their contents in the 21st dynasty, in an attempt to safeguard the royal mummies and to recycle the valuable burial items back into the royal coffers. In the time of Strabo (1st century BCE), Greek tourists were able to visit 40 of the graves. Several graves were reused by Coptic monks, who placed their own inscriptions on the walls. Only the small tomb of Tutankhamun (reigned

1333–23 BCE), positioned on the bottom of the valley and sheltered by a mound of rock chippings thrown down from a later Ramesside tomb, avoided looting.

The spectacular artifacts that were recovered from Tutankhamun's tomb in 1922 and that now live in the Egyptian Museum in Cairo clearly demonstrate how opulent the burial of a great king of the empire's glory must have been. The longest tomb (number 20) belongs to Queen Hatshepsut (reigned c. 1472–58), whose burial chamber is over 700 feet (215 meters) from the entrance and falls 320 feet (100 meters) into the rock.

The biggest and most intricate tomb in the Valley of the Kings (number 5) was presumably erected to hold the burial chambers of several of the sons of Ramses II (reigned 1279–13), the greatest monarch of the 19th dynasty. This tomb, which had been previously identified but rejected as inconsequential, was again rediscovered in the late 1980s and largely excavated in the 1990s. The highest of the tomb's two floors has a central pillared hall and different hallways going out to dozens of rooms.

Carter, Carnarvon and the Discovery of King Tut's Tomb

British archaeologist and Egyptologist Howard Carter together with his backer, Lord Carnarvon, spent many years and a lot of money hunting for a tomb in Egypt's Valley of the Kings that they weren't sure remained. But on November 4, 1922, they discovered it. Carter had unearthed not simply an undiscovered ancient Egyptian tomb, but one that had been largely undisturbed for over 3,000 years. What was inside King Tut's tomb shocked the globe.

Carter had worked in Egypt for 31 years before he unearthed King Tut's tomb. He began his work in Egypt at age 17, utilizing his creative ability to replicate wall pictures and inscriptions. Eight years later (in 1899), Carter was named the Inspector-General of Monuments in Upper Egypt. In 1905, Carter left this employment and in 1907, moved to work for Lord Carnarvon.

George Edward Stanhope Molyneux Herbert, the fifth Earl of Carnarvon, enjoyed racing in the newly created car. But an auto accident in 1901 left him in bad condition. Vulnerable to the west English winter, Lord Carnarvon started spending winters in Egypt in 1903. To pass the time, he took up archaeology as a pastime. Turning up nothing except a mummified cat (still in its coffin) in his first season, Lord Carnarvon decided to recruit someone competent for the future seasons. For this, he recruited Carter.

After three rather successful seasons
working together, World War I brought a
close end to their work in Egypt. Yet, by the
autumn of 1917, Carter and Lord Carnarvon
started digging in earnest in the Valley of
the Kings.

Carter noted that there were numerous
pieces of evidence previously discovered—a
faience cup, a piece of gold foil, and a cache
of funerary goods which all carried the name
of Tutankhamun—that persuaded him that
the tomb of King Tut was yet to be located.
Carter also felt that the positions of these
objects led to a certain region where they
would discover King Tutankhamun's tomb.
Carter was resolved to methodically
examine this region by digging down to the
bedrock.

Besides some old workmen's cottages at the foot of the tomb of Rameses VI and 13 calcite jars at the entrance to the tomb of Merenptah, Carter did not have much to show after five years of excavation in the Valley of the Kings. Thus, Lord Carnarvon decided to cease the hunt. After a chat with Carter, Carnarvon relented and consented to one final season.

Discovery of the tomb

By November 1, 1922, Carter started his last season working in the Valley of the Kings by having his employees reveal the old workmen's cottages at the foot of the tomb of Rameses VI. After uncovering and recording the houses, Carter and his colleagues started to dig the earth underneath them. By the fourth day of effort, they had discovered something—a stair that had been chiseled into the rock.

Work rapidly continued on the afternoon of November 4 until the next morning.

By late afternoon on November 5, 12 steps heading down were visible; and in front of them, stood the top section of a blocked entryway. Carter inspected the painted door for a name. But of the seals that could be read, he discovered only the imprints of the royal necropolis.
To safeguard the discovery, Carter had his employees filled in the steps, hiding them so that none were apparent. While many of Carter's most trusted employees stood watch, Carter went to make arrangements, the first of which was calling Lord Carnarvon in England to deliver the news of the discovery.

It was about three weeks after locating the first step before Carter was able to continue. On November 23, Lord Carnarvon and his daughter, Lady Evelyn Herbert, arrived in Luxor. The next day, the workmen had again cleaned the staircase, now displaying all 16 of its steps and the entire face of the blocked entryway. Now Carter saw something he could not see earlier as the bottom of the doorway had still been covered with rubble: There were multiple seals on the bottom of the entrance with Tutankhamun's name on them.

Now that the door was completely exposed, they saw that the top left of the entryway had been smashed through, likely by tomb thieves, and resealed. The tomb was not intact, although the fact that the tomb had been resealed suggested that the tomb had not been emptied.

A path emerged from the darkness, packed to the brim with limestone pieces. Upon closer investigation, Carter could identify that tomb thieves had excavated a hole through the top left portion of the tunnel because the hole had been repaired in antiquity with bigger, darker boulders than utilized for the remainder of the fill.

This suggested that the tomb had probably been looted twice in antiquity. The first time was within a few years after the king's burial and before there was a sealed door to fill up the corridor. (Scattered artifacts were recovered beneath the fill.) The second time, the burglars had to dig through the fill and could leave only with fewer objects.

The Antechamber

By the next day, the fill along the
26-foot-long corridor had been cleaned
away to disclose another sealed door,
virtually similar to the first. Again, there
were indicators that a hole had been cut in
the entryway and resealed.
Tension increased. If anything was left
inside, it would be a find of a lifetime for

Carter. If the tomb was largely intact, it would be something the world had never seen. The following morning, the plastered door was photographed and the seals noted. Then the door fell, exposing the Antechamber. The wall opposite the entry wall was stacked almost to the ceiling with boxes, chairs, sofas, and so much more—most of them gold—in "ordered chaos."

On the right wall were two life-size sculptures of the king, facing each other as if to guard the blocked entrance that lay between them. This sealed door similarly revealed traces of being broken into and resealed, but this time the thieves had entered through the lower center of the door. To the left of the entryway from the tunnel lay a tangle of pieces from numerous destroyed chariots.

The Annex

As Carter and the others spent time looking at the room and its furnishings, they found another shut door behind the sofas on the far wall. This sealed door likewise had a hole in it, but unlike the others, it has not been resealed. Carefully, they crept behind the sofa and shined their light.

In this room (later dubbed the Annexe), everything was in disarray. Carter hypothesized that authorities had sought to clean up the Antechamber after the thieves had stolen, but they had made no effort to correct the Annexe.

Before the door between the two statues in the Antechamber could be opened, the things in the Antechamber needed to be removed or risk harm to them from flying debris, dust, and movement.

Preservation and Documentation

Carter knew that this job was more than he could accomplish alone, hence he called for and obtained support from a vast number of professionals. To begin the cleaning process, each object was photographed in situ, both with an allocated number and without. Then, a drawing and description of each object were prepared on suitably numbered record cards. Next, the object was marked on a ground plan of the tomb (just for the Antechamber) (only for the Antechamber).

Carter and his team had to be extremely careful when attempting to remove the objects. Since many of the artifacts were in very fragile conditions (such as beaded sandals in which the threads had dissolved, leaving just beads held together by 3,000 years of habit), many things required rapid treatment, such as a celluloid spray, to preserve the items intact for removal.

When an object was successfully removed, it was put onto a stretcher and gauze and other bandages were wrapped around the item to safeguard it for removal. Once a number of stretchers were packed, a team of workers would gently pick them up and transfer them out of the tomb.

As soon as they departed the tomb with the stretchers, they were hailed by hundreds of visitors and media who waited for them at the top. Since news had gone swiftly throughout the globe about the tomb, the popularity of the place was enormous. Every time someone came out of the tomb, cameras would go off.

The trail of stretchers was transported to the conservation laboratory, situated at some distance distant in the tomb of Seti II. Carter had taken this tomb to use as a conservation laboratory, photography studio, carpenter's shop (to manufacture the crates required to convey the artifacts), and a storage. Carter assigned tomb No. 55 as a darkroom.

The antiques, following conservation and documentation, were very carefully packaged into boxes and delivered by train to Cairo. It took Carter and his colleagues seven weeks to clean the Antechamber. On Feb. 17, 1923, they started demolishing the sealed door between the sculptures.

The Burial Chamber

The interior of the Burial Chamber was nearly filled by a massive shrine over 16 feet long, 10 feet broad, and 9 feet tall. The walls of the shrine were composed of gilded wood inlaid with vivid blue china.

Unlike the remainder of the tomb, upon which the walls had been left as a rough-cut rock (unsmoothed and unplastered), the walls of the Burial Chamber were coated with gypsum plaster and painted yellow. Funeral images were painted on these yellow walls.

On the ground near the shrine were a variety of objects, including fragments of two broken necklaces, which seemed as if they had been abandoned by thieves, and enchanted oars "to transport the king's barque [boat] over the seas of the Nether World."

To take apart and study the shrine, Carter had to first destroy the barrier wall between the Antechamber and the Burial Chamber. Still, there were not many areas between the three remaining walls and the shrine. As Carter and his colleagues started to demolish the shrine they realized that this was simply the exterior shrine, with four shrines in all. Each part of the shrines weighed up to half a ton. In the tight confines of the Burial Chamber, labor was arduous and unpleasant.

When the fourth shrine was demolished, the king's sarcophagus was uncovered. The sarcophagus was golden and fashioned out of a single stone of quartzite. The lid did not match the rest of the sarcophagus and had been fractured in the center during antiquity (an effort had been made to disguise the crack by filling it with gypsum) (an attempt had been made to cover the crack by filling it with gypsum).
When the heavy lid was raised, a gilded wooden coffin was revealed. The coffin was of a human form and was 7 feet, 4 inches long.

A year and a half later, conservation work on other artifacts previously retrieved from the tomb had taken priority. Thus, the anticipation of what was underneath was intense.

Inside, they discovered another, smaller casket. The opening of the lid of the second casket revealed a third one, constructed completely of gold. On top of this third and last casket was black stuff that had formerly been liquid and spilled over the coffin from the hands to the ankles. The liquid had solidified over the years and firmly glued the third coffin to the bottom of the second. The heavy residue has to be removed with heat and pounding. Then the lid of the third casket was lifted.

At last, the royal mummy of Tutankhamun was exposed. It had been nearly 3,300 years since a human being had seen the king's remains. This was the first royal Egyptian mummy that has been recovered undamaged since his burial. Carter and the others anticipated King Tutankhamun's mummy would disclose a huge amount of information about ancient Egyptian burial rituals.

Though it was still an extraordinary discovery, Carter and his crew were disappointed to realize that the liquid thrown on the mummy had done a considerable lot of harm. The linen wrappings of the mummy could not be unraveled as intended, but instead had to be removed in huge parts.

Many of the things recovered inside the wrappings had also been damaged, and others were nearly totally dissolved.

Carter and his crew recovered approximately 150 objects on the mummy—almost all of them gold—including amulets, bracelets, collars, rings, and daggers.

The autopsy on the corpse unearthed indicated that Tutankhamun had been around 5 feet 5 1/8 inches tall and had died about age 19.

The Treasury

On the right wall of the Burial Chamber was an entrance into storage, which today is known as the Treasury. The Treasury, like the Antechamber, was stocked with goods including several boxes and model boats. Most noticeable in this area was the huge golden canopic shrine. Inside the gilded shrine was the canopic chest constructed out of a single block of calcite. Inside the canopic chest were the four canopic jars, each in the style of an Egyptian coffin and lavishly painted, housing the pharaoh's embalmed organs: liver, lungs, stomach, and intestines.

Also unearthed in the Treasury were two little coffins located in a basic, undecorated wooden box. Inside these two coffins were the mummies of two preterm fetuses. It is speculated that they were Tutankhamun's children. (Tutankhamun is not known to have had any surviving offspring.)

The Curse

The idea of a young, handsome King of Egypt dying a tragic, untimely death at the hands of a murderous fiend combined with a series of events following the discovery of his tomb created the popular legend of Tut's cursed tomb (popular culture has maintained that those who come into contact with Tut's tomb will die). Although the curse has been discredited numerous times by historians, who think that the basis of the curse tales was bored newsmen covering the excavation of Tut's tomb in conjunction with remarks by the archaeologist Arthur Weigall. Before the discovery of Tut's tomb, mummies were not considered cursed, but magical and healing.

The myth of the curse started with the death of Howard Carter's sponsor, Lord Carnarvon, five months after the discovery of the tomb. He died from an illness as a consequence of a mosquito bite. It is believed that at the same time of his death all of the lights in Cairo went out. Other traditions indicate that Lord Carnarvon's beloved hound dog in England howled and fell dead at the same moment as the Lord's death.

Carnarvon's death provided fire to the myth that there was a curse linked with King Tut's tomb. In total, it took Carter and his colleagues 10 years to record and empty Tutankhamun's tomb. After Carter concluded his work at the tomb in 1932, he proceeded to write a six-volume comprehensive book and died before he was able to finish, dying away at his home in Kensington, London, on March 2, 1939.

Ironically, Tutankhamun, whose obscurity during his own time caused his tomb to be forgotten, has since become one of the most well-known pharaohs of ancient Egypt. Having journeyed across the globe as part of an exhibit, King Tut's corpse now again lies in his tomb in the Valley of the Kings.

King Tut's Family

The family of King Tut is some of the most renowned individuals in Ancient Egyptian history. Their lives were surrounded by turbulent and revolutionary upheavals in Egypt.

Murder, mystery, and intrigue impact the life of the family of King Tut. His father, the heretic King Akhenaten, his stepmother Nefertiti who suddenly vanished, and his Grand Vizier Ay who was also the father of Nefertiti and the grandfather of Ankhesenpaaten, the wife of Tutankhamun. Ankhesenpaaten was compelled to marry her grandpa after Tutankhamun died. She also died under unexplained circumstances. There was much inter-marriage in the family of King Tut. Incest was viewed as an acceptable part of the life of the Egyptian Gods and Goddesses, sustaining the holy lineage.

The Ancient Egyptian creation myth aims to explain how some of the great Egyptian Gods and Goddesses came into existence, their interactions with one another, and the nature and origin of the cosmos. The pharaohs were viewed as living deities hence it was seen as totally normal for them to replicate the incestuous behaviors of the gods.

Father

Known as Amenhotep IV for the first four years of his rule, King Tut's father became known as Akhenaten, the heretic king, in the fifth year of his reign.

He was one of two sons born to Amenhotep III and his Chief Queen Tiye, who ascended the throne following the death of his elder brother.

Although nothing is known about Tut's affection for his father, the ancient Egyptians detested him because he replaced their polytheistic religion with a monotheistic one.
His extremist religious ideas were hoisted onto his citizens by use of the Egyptian army.

All the ancient gods were destroyed and the capital was relocated from Thebes to the new city of Amarna. This disrupted the economy and damaged companies. The opinion among historians is that Akhenaten was so unpopular that he had to abandon his kingship. He died soon after his abdication and the reason for his death has yet to be confirmed. Akhenaten intended to have children with his three eldest daughters, but one of them died during delivery.

Mother

King Tut's mother was once supposed to be a Mitanni princess called Kiya.
However, DNA testing undertaken lately has disproved that assumption and his biological mother is likely to be the "Younger Lady", who is one of the mummies in Akhenaten's tomb.

Kiya was active in court activities until soon before Akhenaten's death and she's commonly described as one of his favorites; her coffin of gilded wood is identical to one of King Tut's.

Since his parents were siblings, Tut's mother was also his aunt and his father was also his uncle.

Queen Nefertiti was his stepmother, as well as his mother-in-law.

She shared Akhenaten's zeal for a monotheistic religion but she was not as hated as he was. Her bust, currently in a museum in Berlin, is one of the most imitated ancient Egyptian works of art and is noted for its realism.

Wife

Ankhesenamun, Tutankhamun's sole wife, was also his half-sister and probably two years younger than him.
They were married after he assumed the kingdom and stayed together till his death. Images of her that have remained reveal that she was a lovely young lady without the deformities and maladies that afflicted her brother.

Both Ankhesenamun and Tutankhamun had the same father, but Ankhesenamen's mother was the lovely Queen Nefertiti. Even though their marriage was planned, the evidence speaks of a happy marriage with pictures of the monarch receiving presents from his bride. They had no surviving successors at the time of Tutankhamun's death, although they had two stillborn daughters. Generations of inbreeding have ultimately resulted in the incapacity to generate viable offspring. Like Tut, her stormy existence was short and brief and her death is unclear.

Other Family Members

Tutankhamun's family members comprised numerous relatives owing to his father's multiple marriages.

Additional family members include:

Smenkhkare- brother

Meritaten- sister

Neferneferuaten

Tasherit- sister

Setepenre- youngest sister

Neferneferure- next to youngest sister

Yuya- great grandfather

Mutemwiya- great grandma

Beketaten- aunt

Nebetah- aunt

Iset- aunt

Henuttaneb- aunt

Sitamun- aunt

Ascension To The Throne

Tutankhamun started his reign as Tutankhaten. He was raised in the royal harem, marrying his sister at an early age. At this period Ankhesenamun was known as Ankhesenpaaten. At the age of nine, he was anointed pharaoh at Memphis. He reigned between 1332 and 1323 BC. The change in the names of the young pharaoh and his bride is a consequence of the choice to revert Egypt to an ancient religious practice of worship Amun instead of Aten. This reconciled the young couple with those who represented the previous order of religion.

The bulk of the construction undertaken on temples and shrines during the reign of Tutankhamun remained incomplete. Later pharaohs finished the construction and changed Tut's name with their own.

For example, the Luxor temple in Thebes exhibits works performed under Tutankhamun's tenure. After Tut's death, Horemheb's name replaced Tut's name on the temple, but the old version is still evident in certain sections.

Legacy

As a monarch, Tutankhamun was widely regarded. This may have arisen from the great animosity people felt toward his father, but the young king would probably have been popular anyway. Although many pharaohs were regarded as gods after their death, Tutankhamun was adored in this fashion while he was still alive. Many of the choices taken under Tutankhamun were made by his supervisor (and ultimately successor) Ay, the general Horemheb, and the treasury Maya.

In the second year of Tut's leadership, he transferred the capital of Egypt from Akhenaten to Thebes and relegated the deity Aten to a seldom mentioned divinity. He commissioned a variety of big architectural projects, including the clever choice of a massive temple to the deity Amun — a large public statement that he was renouncing the beliefs his father had pushed on the Egyptian people.

The kingdom was weak politically and economically after 12 years under Akhenaten and Tutankhamun was able to restore Egypt to its previous splendor.

Mysterious Death

When King Tut's mummy was originally
recovered, researchers detected injuries to
the corpse. His unusual demise rapidly led
to several speculations including intrigue
and murder among the Egyptian royals. The
initial exams by Howard Carter and a team
headed by Dr. Douglas Derry could not
reach a firm decision on the cause of death.

The majority of Egyptologists thought that
his death happened from a fall from a
chariot or other similar mishap.
Recently, an international study team under
the supervision of Dr. Chris Naunton found
injuries on one side of Tutankhamun's
corpse, which led to the conclusion that
King Tut was engaged in a chariot collision,

but subsequent analysis revealed that this was exceedingly implausible.

The hunt for a medical reason for death has revealed much about the life of Tutankhamun. He probably never enjoyed good health during his life. Scans indicate he suffered from a bone condition paired with a club foot. Researchers think Tut required canes to walk. This explains the 139 ebony, ivory, silver, and gold canes discovered inside his grave.

Despite being a monarch god-king of Egypt, he also faced the same fate as many of his subjects: malaria. His physique reveals symptoms of having undergone multiple malarial episodes throughout his brief life.

One of these infections, malaria tropica, is
one of the most frequent types of the illness.

The Funeral

The burial of Tutankhamun, while identical
to any funeral in ancient Egypt, contained
far more expensive elements owing to his
prominence as the pharaoh of Egypt.
Scholars think it to have taken place
sometime between February and April. The
embalming procedure was the longest,
thought to require many weeks. Embalmers
removed the internal organs (buried in
canopic jars together with the dead), then
dried the corpse with natron. They then
administered a treatment of unguents,
herbs, and resin - a greater variety of
ointments than the poorer classes would
have been able to purchase. The corpse of

the child pharaoh was then draped in exquisite linen, not just to preserve his body, but also to mold it for the afterlife - the body that would live eternally.

Archaeologists uncovered remnants of the embalming procedure in the area of Tutankhamun's tomb. This shows that, maybe, ancient Egyptians felt they maintained a trace of the buried individual. Vessels for water, albeit some little and weak, made with symbolic intent, are evidence for burial rituals of cleansing. The tomb also contained a variety of dishes, bowls, and plates that stored food and drink offerings. These were buried with the pharaoh, so he would utilize them in the afterlife.

King Tut's burial comprised elaborate adornments of his tomb: mural murals, chariots and daily objects for the afterlife, and magnificent gold jewels. There are also incredibly well-preserved relics of flora used for ornamental reasons - olive branches, picris, rennet, and blue cornflowers.

Ten years of labor documenting the vast quantity of objects indicated that Tut's burial occurred fast in chambers smaller than normal given the magnitude of his riches.

King Tutankhamun's tomb was just 12.07 feet high, 25.78 feet broad and 101.01 feet long. Inside were nearly 3,000 distinct artifacts, mostly of pure gold. The antechamber was in full disorder. Golden furnishings and disassembled chariots lay strewn into the area. The addition included more furnishings and jars of oil, ointments, food, and alcohol.

The burial room included the gilded layers of Tut's coffin and the famed death mask. A treasured area, guarded by a statue of the deity Anubis, housed jeweled chests, expensive jewelry, model boats, and a golden shrine with the Canopic jars carrying King Tut's internal organs. Historians think that Egyptian priests buried Tutankhamun inside his tomb before the paint had time to dry on the walls. Microbial growth detected on the walls of the tomb reveals to experts that the paint was still wet when the tomb was walled off from the world. Dark areas found on the tomb's artwork are a consequence of microbial development and are now regarded as a distinctive feature.

The tiny rooms, hasty burial and ancient efforts at tomb robbing explain the chaotic circumstances observed inside the tomb. It seems most probable that Tut's successor, Ay, hurried his burial to seamlessly take over the reign of Egypt.

Strife for the Throne

Tut's widow, Ankhesenamun, was in a perilous situation following his death. She was the last remaining member of Akhenaten's family and was left alone as the monarch of Egypt. She was young and surrounded by highly ambitious older guys. Letters suggest that she sought to rescue her husband's heritage and her seat on the throne by contacting the King of the Hittites. She requested him to send her a spouse as protection. Otherwise, she says she will be compelled to marry a servant.

The prince started his voyage, but mysterious assassins assassinated him before he arrived. Ankhesenamun then married the heavenly father Ay who governed Egypt for four years, only to be replaced by General Horemheb.

Glittering Treasures of Tutankhamun

Once inside the tomb, Carter discovered halls loaded with wealth. This contained sculptures, gold jewelry, Tutankhamun's mummy, chariots, model boats, canopic jars, seats, and paintings. It was an astonishing find and one of the most significant made in the history of archeology. As told, there were almost 5,000 artifacts in the tomb. It took Carter and his crew 10 years to record everything. Below are some of the king's riches.

Golden Funeral Mask

This golden mask portrays King Tut as a physical ideal. The beard on the mask was believed to have been broken and detached, then quickly put together with epoxy. The Egyptians refute the evidence, but the unmistakable line is there for everyone to see. The beard portrayed was the norm for all monarchs, whether male and female. The beards were ceremonial and stylized, being

worn as a costume rather than growing
organically.

Wooden Guardian Statue of the King

This life-sized statue of Tutankhamun, with
piercing golden eyes, gilded attire and
contrasting black skin, was one of two
sentries that Howard Carter uncovered
guarding the locked door to Tut's burial
chamber.

Beetle mania

This piece of jewellery contains a scarab beetle made of lapis lazuli, a semi-precious stone treasured for its deep blue hue, making it a favourite for Ancient Egyptian jewellery. The scarab was considered holy; Khepri was the scarab-faced deity of the rising Sun and rebirth.

Gilded Wooden Bed

Experts say this gold-covered bed was created for King Tut's burial. The Ancient Egyptians thought that the dead were only sleeping and that they woke up when they were reincarnated in the afterlife. To secure the Pharaoh's safe journey into the afterlife and to keep bad forces at bay, heavenly images were carved on to the bed — in this example Bes, a deity who scared away evil spirits from newborn newborns, and Tauret, the hippo goddess.

Miniature Canopic Coffin

The afterlife was very significant to the Ancient Egyptians. They thought that by preserving a deceased person's body – via the process of mummification – the spirit would go on in the afterlife eternally. During the mummification process, the internal organs were removed, wrapped in linen bandages and stored in receptacles called canopic vessels. Usually they were jars, but occasionally the organs were preserved in little golden coffins. This exquisite casket housed King Tut's organs.

The crook and flail

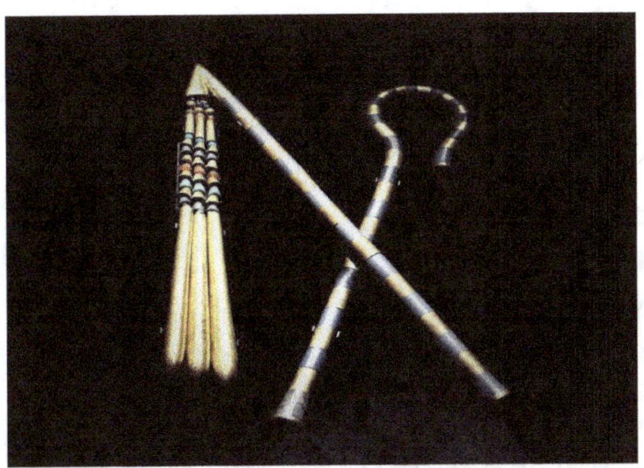

The crook and flail were the main emblems of royal authority in Ancient Egypt — the shepherd's crook signifying royalty and the flail the fertility of the land. This specific sample was discovered among the wrappings of Tutankhamun's mummy. The crossed hands are composed of gold with coloured glass while the crook and flail have silver centers.

Silver military trumpet

Two trumpets were unearthed within the tomb of Tutankhamun. It is thought that the trumpets are magical. The first time one was blown following its re-discovery, the lights went out in Cairo's Egyptian Museum — and a few months later war broke out in Europe. The trumpets were played again before the Six Day War in 1967, before the 1990 Gulf War and the Egyptian revolution in 2011.

Some individuals have attributed these bizarre coincidences to the curse.

Golden sandal

Made from pure gold for burial usage, these sandals would have been put on the deceased Pharaoh's feet before he was wrapped in strips of linen. They resemble leather and plant sandals Tutankhamun would have worn in life. The function of the sandal-bearer to a pharaoh was one of the most significant occupations in Ancient Egyptian culture. As well as carrying a pharaoh's footwear, they would also wash the royal feet.

Statute of Anubis

Anubis was the jackal which guided the souls of the Egyptian deceased into the underworld. Associated with the practice of mummification, the canine was regarded to be an excellent guard

The Mummified Body Of King Tut

The last and by far the most essential object housed in the tomb is the monarch himself. The corpse has been inspected by medical professionals and their judgment was that he was little and most likely unwell.

Interesting Facts About King Tut

For thousands of years, it appeared his legacy was lost to the sands of time. It was only after the 1922 discovery of his tomb that he became the most renowned Egyptian of all.

Here are 14 amazing facts about Tutankhamun, the 'boy king'.

- Tutankhamun was buried with 130 walking sticks to aid with his clubbed foot, which he regularly wore orthopaedic sandals for. These sandals contained drawings of his opponents on the soles, so he could always stomp on his foes. He had enormous front incisors and a significant overbite, a trait of his family.

- He has the smallest royal tomb in the Valley of the Kings
- He loved to hunt ostriches, feeling pleased when he returned with his prey. He was buried with an ostrich fan which would have contained 42 alternating brown and white feathers. Although these feathers deteriorated long ago, the handle portrays the monarch heading forth in his chariot to hunt, and on the reverse, returning in victory with his catch.
- Since Howard Carter's discovery of the tomb, experts have done a DNA test of the king's remains, enabling them to establish a family tree extending back five generations.
- Tutankhamun's father, Akhenaten, was a religious extremist who

transformed the whole religion of ancient Egypt to the worship of deity Aten. He also erected a new capital, devoted to Aten and called it Amarna.

- Tutankhamun wasn't born to Nefertiti who had daughters only, causing tension in the royal court.
- Tutankhamun's favorite possession was an iron dagger, named "iron from the sky."
- Tutankhamun had a dog as a pet and dog staff were found in his tomb.
- Tutankhamun was trained in the military and was great at archery.
- His successors tried to erase him from history.
- He was entombed with a meteorite dagger. The dagger was found on the corpse of the mummy when he was

discovered, but it wasn't until a few years ago that portable x-ray fluorescence spectrometry confirmed that the materials originated from space.

- When his tomb was unearthed in the early 20th century, King Tut had a significant effect on pop culture. The Egyptian style invaded the 1920s, appearing in fashion, home design, and architecture.
- By performing a virtual autopsy of his corpse using CT scan data, scientists were able to generate a 3D image of what King Tut may have looked like when he was alive 3000 years ago.
- Senet, one of the world's oldest board games, was discovered inside King Tut's tomb.

www.ingramcontent.com/pod-product-compliance
Lightning Source LLC
Chambersburg PA
CBHW070553160726
48003CB00005B/2035